The Science of Rondo

"Progressions, Variations & Transitions"

By Marcus DiBernardo

Part of "The Method" Soccer Coaching Series

February 2014

The Science of Rondo

"Progressions, Variations & Transitions"

I was introduced to rondo some twenty years ago as a player, however no one told me it was called "rondo" nor did they explain the objectives of the game. At the time there were actually coaches preaching what an unrealistic training exercise rondo was. They believed it taught the direct opposite of what you want your players to do because after passing the player stood still—it did not teach *movement* off the ball. In college we played rondo once a in a great while and only as a fun activity before training actually started. There was no intensity level or understanding of its real purpose. To us it was just a keep away game with no real purpose. Now, twenty-three years later, as a seasoned head coach I have a totally new appreciation and understanding of rondo, which I'd like to share with you!

Let's start off with a few quotes from famous players who used rondo to develop into some of the world's best players.

"Everything that goes on in a match, except shooting, you can do in a rondo. The competitive aspect, fighting to make space, what to do when in possession and what to do when you haven't got the ball, how to play 'one touch' soccer, how to counteract the tight marking and how to win the ball back." ~**Johan Cruyff** (Legendary player for FC Barcelona and Holland)

"It's all about rondos. Rondo, rondo, rondo. Every single day. It's the best exercise there is. You learn responsibility and not to lose the ball. If you lose the ball, you go in the middle. Pum-pum-pum-pum, always one touch. If you go in the middle, it's humiliating, the rest applaud and laugh at you." ~**Xavi** (One of the best midfielders in FC Barcelona and Spain's history)

Rondo Defined:

If I had to define "Rondo" it would be as follows: Rondo is a training game in which the group who is possession has a numerical advantage. Rondo can be as little as 3 v 1 to 10 v 2 over another group of players. The objective of the group in possession is to keep the ball away from the defenders, while the defenders objective is to win the ball.

Rondo is different than other possession drills because the players take up a pre-set space in the circle rather than roaming all over. Many possession drills will have players move to spaces that relate more to the movements of a regular game. However, some of the rondo variations do involve movements out of the pre-set typical rondo spaces.

Rondos develop players in the following ways:

Decision Making & Number of Touches: Players need to think very quickly in rondo as the ball can move very fast. Being a step ahead and having good vision is required to maintain possession. The number of touches a player gets in rondo is high. In a typical 11 v 11 game players touch the ball between 20 and 40 times. In rondo they can have the same number of touches in 5 minutes. The more meaningful touches, the more a player will improve.

Technique, Mobility & Agility: In order to keep possession the players must have a good level of technical ability. Pep Guardiola the former FC Barcelona Coach would talk about playing on the edge your technical ability, while still maintaining possession with solid technique. The faster the ball moves in rondo the faster the players need to execute. This includes being balanced, mobile, quick, agile, technical and making quick decisions.

Teamwork and Collective Understanding: Rondo is not an individual game. It requires teamwork to possess the ball. It also requires teamwork of the defending players to win the ball back therefore; the understanding between the players is enhanced as they begin to work as one unit.

Problem Solving & Creativity: Problem solving in soccer is the name of the game! Can players find solutions to break down the opposition's defense? Rondo tests the player's ability to problem solve the entire time. Being creative can often help break down a defense.

Competition: Rondo is an enjoyable fun environment that creates an atmosphere of healthy competition. Competition pushes players to train at higher intensities and elevate their game.

Is Rondo An Overnight Fast Track to Success?

It is very important to understand that Rondo does not build skill overnight. In fact, the midfielder Xavi explains that the secret to rondo is not found out in one week, one month or one year. You get more and more out of rondo the more you train rondo. Players have to hit certain levels of skill to fully reap all the benefits of rondo and that can literally take years. At FC Barcelona, players normally do between 1,500 and 1,800 hours of rondo between ages 6 to 20. Deliberate practice states that 80% of the training should focus on 20% of the most important skills. It is obvious that Barcelona places a very high value on rondo. I understand that not many teams can play like Barcelona but the ability to possess the ball in tight spaces against high intensity opponents can be useful for any team.

Here are key terms to remember when playing rondo:

First Line Break/Pass – pass to the person next to you. Easiest pass to make in rondo. Does not require a wide range of vision.

Second Line Break/Pass - The pass will bypass the person next to you but does not split defenders. The second line pass requires a little larger passing vision. This is slightly more difficult than the first line pass.

Third Line Split Pass - This is a ball is the money ball that splits the defenders through the middle. This pass requires the most skill, creativity, vision and timing to pull off. In soccer the ultimate goal is to get the ball forward and score. Third line split passes help develop this skill.

Key Points for All Rondo Training:

I will not put these key points down for every rondo drill in the book. However, these key points will most likely apply to every rondo drill. Remember these key points!

Key Points:

1. Stay on the balls of your feet with an open stance ready to receive the ball from any side or forward direction and pass the ball to any side or forward option (forward angle passes as well).
2. Always be focused and mentally into the game. Try to get into a high-level zone of performance and concentration.
3. Try to think one or two steps ahead of the play. Speed of thought equals speed of play.
4. Have fun and bring energy to the group. There is nothing wrong with having tons of fun if the training is of the highest quality.
5. Let your teammates know when they did well or when they need to pick it up. Clap and shout to celebrate the great passes and defensive plays! Teams that demand a high level of performance from each player get better faster.
6. Speed of play, creativity, teamwork, sound technique and problem solving are all very important.

7. The importance of keeping possession as an individual and team is the primary objective but look for *Third Line Splitting Passes* when they present themselves. Forward passing is what scores goals and those opportunities need to be taken when they are available.
8. Establish a rhythm to the passing. The tempo of play and rhythm is critical for success.

How I Teach Rondo:

Here is a brief explanation of the way I teach rondo. First, my team plays rondo every single day in one form or another. We are always changing up numbers, rules, grid sizes and variations of the game. The goal is to get players problem solving and thinking by changing the variables. Our program places a lot of value on teaching players to be thinkers and problem solvers. The more a player develops their cognitive ability in training the more of an intelligent soccer player they become. Changing the rondos also helps with eliminating the feeling of "oh this again". The progressions, variations and transitions really help keep players stay intense and motivated. My next experiment is to have my team play rondo in the sand! Have fun with the rondos and see what works best for your team. I would like to hear your feedback after you implement the new rondo ideas!

Feel free to contact me with any questions or thoughts. I can be emailed directly from my blog at www.coachdibernardo.com. Also, be sure to check out my book "*The Method*" *Redefining the Art of Soccer Coaching and Management*. Keep an eye out for future "The Method" Books coming out soon as well. You can buy the method online at Amazon. http://www.amazon.com/dp/B00HYHL9OI

Exercise One

Fundamental Rondo

Players: 7v2

For basic rondo a 10 yard x 10 yard grid is fine for 6v2 all the way up to 9v2. For smaller numbers like 3v1, 4v1 or 4v2 make the grid a tiny bit smaller. I prefer tighter spaces if the players can handle it. If you see players are having a lot of difficulty keeping the ball make the grid bigger, increase the number of touches allowed, and even eliminate one of the defenders. It may take some time, but eventually players will become more skilled at rondo and keeping rhythm in possession will be possible.

Grid: 10 yards x 10 yards in which players form circle. They can go outside the grid a foot or so but the idea is to keep the circle shape and not make the circle larger.

Key Points & Objectives

Stay on the balls of your feet with an open stance ready to receive the ball from both sides or from a forward direction while being able to pass the ball to both sides or forward. Always be focused and mentally into the game. Try to get into a high level zone of play and concentration. Begin to think one or two steps ahead of the play. Have fun and bring energy to the group. Let your teammates know when they did well or when they need to pick it up. Clap and shout out the great passes and defensive plays! Speed of play, creativity, teamwork, sound technique and problem solving are all very important. The importance of keeping possession as an individual and team is a primary objective but look for *Third Line Splitting Passes* when they present themselves. It is very important to keep a high passing tempo while finding a rhythm to the possession. The book is going to cover many variations but remember rondo is usually played one or two touch.

Fundamental Rondo:

Exercise Two

Breaking The Lines Rondo

Players: 6v2 to 9v2 recommended

Grid: 10 yards x 10 yards in which players form circle. They can go outside the grid a foot or so but the idea is to keep the circle shape and not make the circle larger.

Key Points & Objectives

Players must play the pass through one line with every pass.

The pass has to cross a line before it is received by another teammate.

Players are forced to increase their passing vision when lines are removed in the progressions. The game becomes harder with the removal some lines.

Note: The set-up works better with tape or string/rope on the floor to create the zones. You can use cones to define the outside grid space. The ball needs to roll freely over the zones so cones do not work well for marking inside lines.

Breaking The Lines Exercise A) Notice the circle is split into six zones.

Breaking The Lines Rondo Exercise B) Notice the circle is now only split into four zones. This is the logical next progression to Exercise A.

Exercise Three

Moving Rondo

Players: 5v2 to 9v2 recommended

Grid: 10 yards x 10 yards in which players form circle. They can go outside the grid a foot or so but the idea is to keep the circle shape and not make the circle larger. The variations below will need two grids than four next to each other.

Key Points & Objectives:

Players look to complete four passes and then play their teammates into the open grid. The group at the point all has to run into the open grid following the pass. Players do not have to run keeping the shape of a circle. Once they get into the next grid they can regain the shape of the circle and look to complete four passes again before sending ball into the open grid. The players in possession can make more than four passes in the same grid but they can't play in the open grid before four passes are completed. You can change the number of passes and players to adjust for skill level. This is a high energy and free flowing game of rondo that the players enjoy.

Moving Rondo Exercise A) One Team with Two Grids

Moving Rondo Exercise B) Two Teams with Four Grids

Exercise Four

Two Team Color Coded Rondo

Players: 4v2 to 9v2

Grid: 10 yards x 10 yards in which players form circle. They can go outside the grid a foot or so but the idea is to keep the circle shape and not make the circle larger. This exercise requires two grids with 5-10 yards separation. You can set-up grids side-by-side or diagonally from one another.

Key Points & Objectives:

One grid will be playing 8v2 for example. The other grid will be passing the ball in circle with no defenders. Every player in the game has a partner. Partners wear the same color bib/vest. You can do five or six colors and even repeat some colors. If the defenders win the ball the person who gave the ball away and his partner must run to the other grid and be the defenders. This is very challenging because defenders may be running from behind you into the circle looking to steal the ball. Players must be scanning and always looking around to see where the pressure may be coming from. The energy and intensity levels in this version are always very good. Players do not want to let their partners down or stay in the middle pressuring the ball that long.

Two Team Color Coded Rondo

Exercise Five
Moving Circle Rondo

Players: 5v2 to 10v2

Grid: 10 yards long x 25 yards in width. Players should make the regular 10x10 circle leaving 15 yards space to side.

Key Points and Objectives:

The group must try and keep the ball as the circle moves together until they reach the end of the 25yard width. If they are still in possession the group should try and travel back the other direction. The actual game of rondo is played like exercise one. If a player gives the ball away he changes with the defender quickly by tossing them the bib (bibs always held in hand and not worn). Some people like to switch both defenders but unless you have even numbers I see no need to. Moving rondo gives the players a collective problem to solve. They must work together to be successful.

Moving Circle Rondo

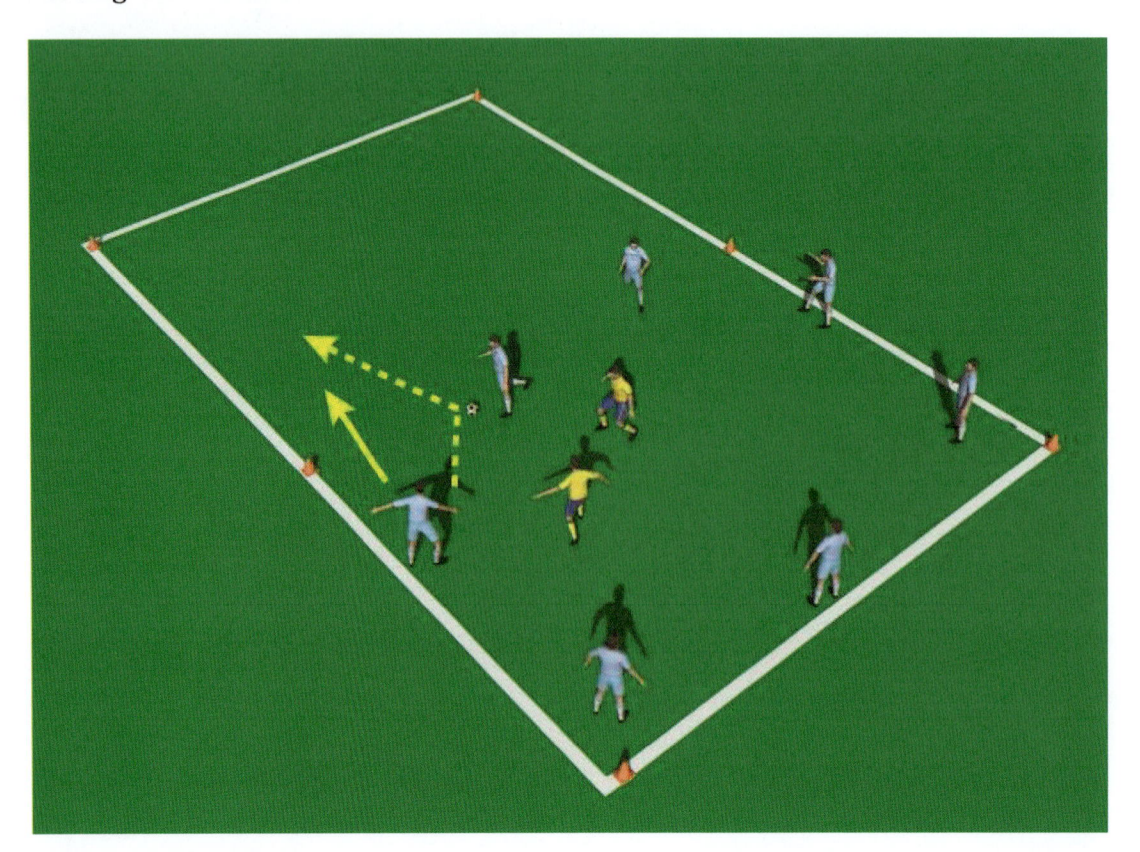

Exercise Six
Line Passing Rondo

Players: 6v2 to 10v2

Grid: 10 yards x 10 yards in which players form circle. They can go outside the grid a foot or so but the idea is to keep the circle shape and not make the circle larger.

Key Points & Objectives:

The coach will instruct the group in first line and second line passes. Game One: Players are not allowed to make any first line passes (can not pass to person next to you) only second and third line passes. Game Two: After any first line pass the next pass must be second line or third line. Feel free to throw in your own rules and variables. This game works very well to increase concentration in rondo while increasing passing vision, speed of play and thought. Use the same rules as fundamental rondo.

Line Passing Rondo

Exercise Seven

Rondo To Possession To Rondo

Players: Two Circles of 3v1 to 10v2

Grid: Two grids 10 yards x 10 yards in which players form circle. The grids should be separated by 5-10 yards. Players can go outside the grid a foot or so but the idea is to keep the circle shape and not make the circle larger. Both grids need to be inside a bigger square grid. The size of the larger big square depends on the total number of players being used. A 35x35 larger grid for a total of 18 players is a starting point.

Key Points & Objectives:

Example: Rondo Grid #1 10x10 - will have 7 Red players and 2 yellow defending players. Rondo Grid #2 10x10 - will have 7 Blue players and 2 yellow defending players. The defenders do not change in the middle for the rondo. After two rotations of the exercise you can switch the yellows out. Let the two grids play rondo for 2-3 minutes and then call "Combined Play". This will mean the 7 Red will play against the 7 Blue with the 4 Yellow being neutral players who help the team in possession. The game is two touch and players can go anywhere in the larger square grid which can be around 35x35 for 18 players. After 1 minute the coach will say "rondo" the teams will go quickly back to their own rondo grids and to continue their rondo play.

Rondo To Possession To Rondo

Exercise Eight

Rondo Transitions To Passing Patterns, Technical Training and Fitness

Players: For these variations it depends on how many players per group you want to use and what you are transitioning back and forth to. Groups can be 3v1 to 10v2.

Grid: 10 yards x 10 yards in which players form circle. They can go outside the grid a foot or so but the idea is to keep the circle shape and not make the circle larger.

Key Points & Objectives: The basic idea here is to get creative with the transition between rondo and another training drill that makes sense. I like to transition from rondo to either passing patterns or fitness. I set up the grids close together so the transition is quick. When the Coach calls "rondo" the players engage in rondo and when "passing" or "fitness" is called the group rotates to those drills. I like to time these, so I typically spend 3 minutes rondo and 3 minutes passing patterns or fitness. You can design it the anyway you like. The important part is that there is little down time in transition and players are always training focused and well.

Rondo To Passing Patterns

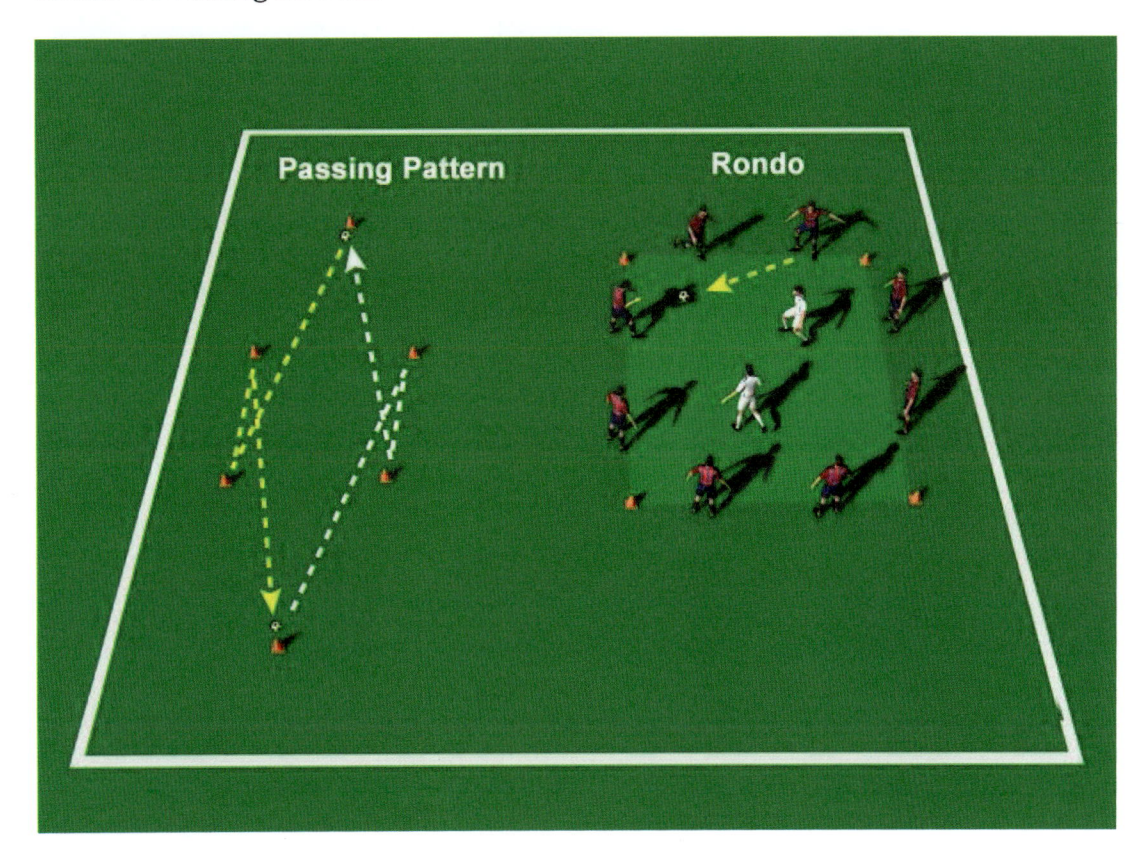

Rondo To Fitness

Exercise Nine

Sliding Player Rondo

Players: 5v2 to 9v2

Grid: 10 yards x 10 yards in which players form circle. They can go outside the grid a foot or so but the idea is to keep the circle shape and not make the circle larger.

Key Points & Objectives:

Sliding rondo is simply rondo with a player who can slide into the middle and help keep the ball with the rest of the team. The middle player can either stay the entire time or take turns sliding in and out of the middle at any time. I like having the middle player sliding in and out as another player takes his spot in fluid motion without the game being stopped. It adds another layer of complexity and teamwork to the exercise.

Sliding Player Rondo

Exercise Ten

Rondo Variations

Players: It depends on the variation you are using for the rondo.

Grid: 10 yards x 10 yards in which players form circle. They can go outside the grid a foot or so but the idea is to keep the circle shape and not make the circle larger.

Key Points & Objectives:

These variations can be worked into rondo training to make the players problem solve, adapt and find solutions.

A) Follow your pass: For 7v2 to 10v2 rondo have players follow their pass and move to the persons position you just passed the ball to. Encourages movement after passing.

B) Do a push up after passing: This makes it impossible for the person you just passed the ball to give it right back to you (you are doing your push up and are not ready to receive the pass). This reduces players passing options making them adapt quickly.

C) Sprint back to a cone that is 5 yards behind each player in the circle: This does the same as the push up but it works on running fitness instead of upper body strength.

D) Two touch both feet mandatory: This makes players receive with one foot and pass with the other. It leads to using both feet and playing in a quick 1-2 rhythm.

E) Players must hold hands in circle: This makes the grid smaller and ball movement picks up speed. Teamwork and speed of play are needed.

F) Mandatory cheering after six completed passes or split: This creates a fun energetic atmosphere and team bonding. It is a nice variation to get players to enjoy the training environment.

G) Air Rondo: Start with the ball in the air, it can't touch the ground. This is a high level very skilled form of rondo.

H) Add up to four defenders in the middle as you increase outside numbers and inside possession player (grid would have to be enlarger)

Exercise Eleven

9v4 Rondo

Players: 13

Grid: 35x25 yards

Key points and Objectives:

The blue team has 6 players positioned on the outside of the grid and 3 inside the grid. The red team has 4 players inside the grid. Start the game allowing all players two-touches. If the red team wins the ball, they play 4v3 inside the grid, as the outside 6 blue players must stay on the outside. Once the inside 3 blue players win the ball back, they can use the outside 6 blue players to keep possession. As the group becomes more skilled, reduce the blue teams touches to one-touch. Variations include outside players one-touch and inside payers two touch, all players one touch would be the highest level.

9v4 Rondo

Exercise Twelve

Cognitive Rondo: Ball Toss

Players: 12

Grid: 10x10 yards

Key points and Objectives:

This game is the same as fundamental rondo but with a change. Start with one soccer ball or tennis ball that a selected player will hold in their hands. The player must toss the ball to another player while rondo is being played to another player. The ball is continuously tossed (underhand) as long rondo is being played. The players are now forced to concentrate on two separate tasks at the same time. They must be aware of two tasks, the ball being tossed and the rondo being played. Players are forced to process information non-stop in cognitive rondo. The game can be played 10v2 to start with one ball being tossed. Once the players become better at the game add another ball to be tossed and caught. In the diagram the yellow circles represent the balls to be tossed.

Cognitive Rondo: Ball Toss

Exercise Thirteen

Cognitive Rondo: No Same Color Passing

Players: 12

Grid: 10x10 yards

Key points and Objectives:

The set-up is the same as fundamental rondo using a 10v2 shape. The 2 defenders in the middle are holding tennis balls in their hands. This lets the other players know they are the defenders. If a player gives possession away, the defender simply tosses the incoming player the tennis ball. The tennis ball simply replaces the tossing of the bib (tennis ball identifies the defenders). There are 6 different pairs of players in this game. Each pair is wearing a different color bib/vest than the other pairs. The rule of the game is players are not allowed to pass to the same color (their teammate). Your teammate might be next to you, on the other side of the circle or playing defense. It is crucial players identify the location of their teammate at all times. This will require players to think quickly and process additional information in order to be successful. Variation: require players to switch positions with the person they passed the ball to. This will make players continuously have to scan to locate their partner.

Cognitive Rondo: No Same Color Passing:

Exercise Fourteen

Rondo to 10v2 One Touch

This is the first of two drills I recommend to transition to once you finish rondo. These drills compliment what the players were doing in rondo and the transition it virtually seamless. I added these because my players really enjoy them and seem to get a lot out of them.

Players: 9v2 or 10v2 or with less numbers go 6v1 to 8v1.

Grid: 10 yards x 10 yards. No player allowed outside the grid. It is important to keep the space tight and only 10x10.

Key Points & Objectives:

The game is 1 touch only. Players should not be in a circle like rondo. They need to be moving inside the grid all the time on the balls of their feet ready to play one touch. The two defenders have the bibs/vests in their hands and try to win the ball. If a defender wins the ball or it goes outside the grid he throws the bib to the players who gave the ball away. The game should not be stopping. Have a coach outside feeding balls in right away as soon as the ball is hit out of the grid. Arsenal FC uses this drill and it is one of my personal favorites. It teaches quick play, one touch passing and movement off the ball. This 10v2 one touch game is played in the same 10x10 grid as your rondo so the transition is seamless.

10v2 One Touch

Exercise Fifteen

Game Related Rondo Transition

This next exercise is very closely related to the real 11v11 game. The rondo skills can be directly used and seen in this game.

Players: 17-18 players

Grid: 35 yards long x 25 yards wide. You can feel free to change the grid size depending on your objectives. If you want the players to be under a lot of pressure then keep the grid small, if you want them to run a bit more then make the grid larger. Experiment and see what you like.

Key Points & Observations:

This is a touch two game with players set up in position specific spaces on the field. Each team has two center backs, two outside wing backs, defensive center mid, passing center mid, attacking center mid and a forward. There is also one neutral player on the field playing for the team in possession. The neutral player helps the ball move swiftly. The objective is to move the ball from your backs through the midfield and to your forward. Once the forward receives the ball, the team will attempt to move the ball back to the defenders without losing possession. Once possession is lost, players must work hard to get the ball back. Both teams are set up the exact same way trying to accomplish the same tasks. Outside players are located in safe zones so inside players can't come out of the field and take the ball from outside players. The teams on the inside can only play to their own players on the outside. The ball moves very fast in this game, it is directly game related and many of the rondo skills will be used. If you are playing two grids of rondo of 7v2 the transition is simple to this game and quick. The transition form rondo to this game can be 90 seconds if everything is planned out well.

Game Related Rondo Drill

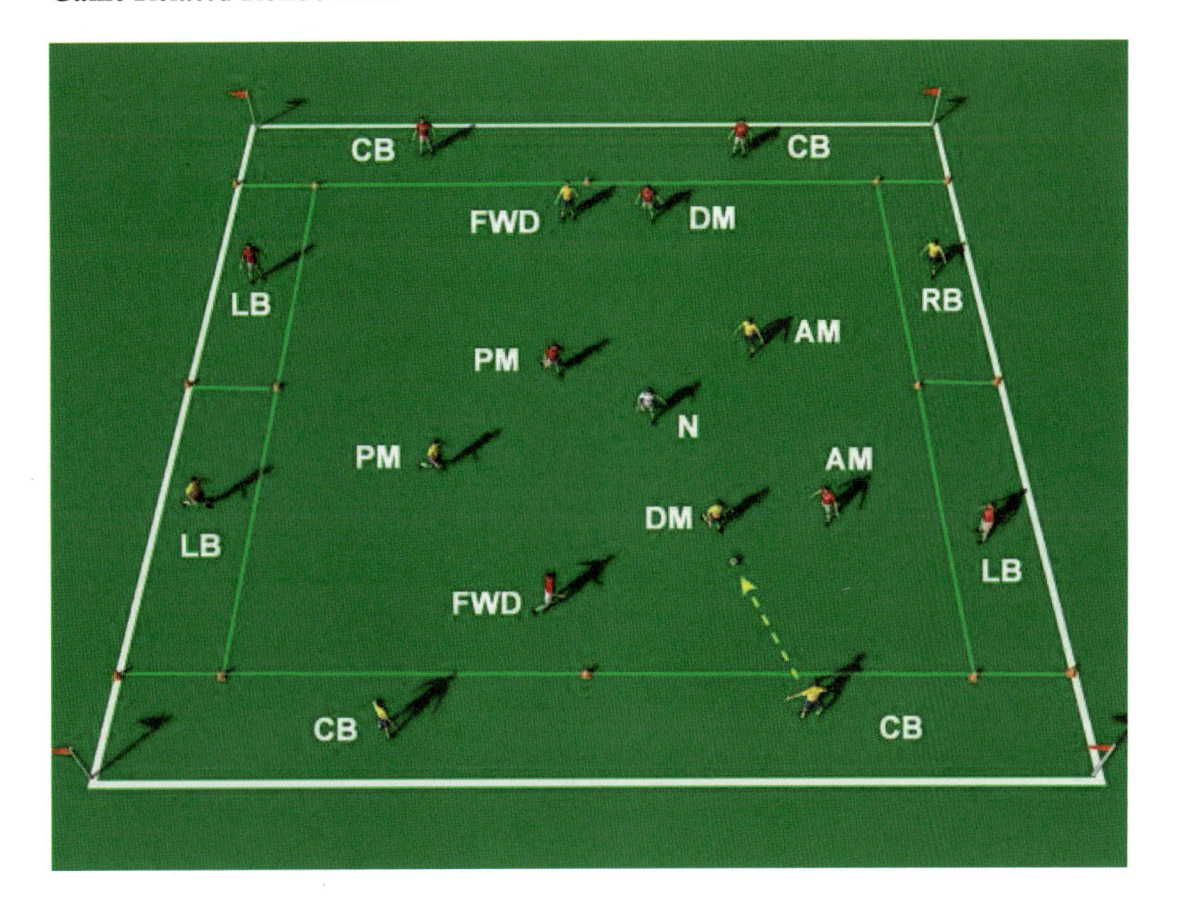

I hope you find the rondo progressions and variations useful. I would like to thank John, Mickey, Curt and Jay my fellow coaches who have contributed to my soccer education.

Remember, don't be afraid to experiment and create new variations. You can always contact me through my blog at www.coachdibernardo.com - I am happy to answer any questions!

Also feel free to check out my other books:

The Method - The Art of Coaching & Managing Soccer

The Science of Rondo - Progressions, Variations and Transitions

Professional Soccer Finishing Drills

Professional Soccer Passing Patterns

45 Professional Soccer Possession Drills: Top Drills From The World's Top Clubs

The Science of Soccer Team Defending

Soccer Smart

References and Sources:

"Our Competition is the World: Ideas for implementing the United States Soccer Curriculum." By Stan Baker, 2012. Lulu Publishing.

"The Talent Code" By Daniel Coyle. May 2009. Published By Bantam Dell. NY, NY.

"Coaching The Tiki Taka Style Of Play", By Jed C. Davies. November 2013. Published By Soccertutor.com

Printed in Great Britain
by Amazon.co.uk, Ltd.,
Marston Gate.